D1401317

# Heartfelt Thank Yous

## PERFECT WAYS FOR BRIDES
## TO SAY THANK YOU

BY

BEVERLY CLARK

WILSHIRE PUBLICATIONS

Published by Wilshire Publications

Distributed by:
Publishers Group West, Emeryville, CA

*Cover Design: Victoria Torf Fulton*
*Cover Photography: Henry Hamamoto*
*Book Design: Robin La Fevers*
*Illustrations: Itoko Maeno*
*Typography and Layout: Cirrus Design*
*Editor: Gail M. Kearns*

Special thanks to Contstance Kay Inc.
for use of their "Little Piece of Art" by Doré

ISBN: 0-934081-19-0

*To everyone who struggles to find
just the right word.*

# CONTENTS

# INTRODUCTION

*E*TIQUETTE, the accepted guidelines for behavior in polite society, is not as rigid as we might think. Like the language we use to communicate, it is a dynamic, evolving process. As the composition and interaction of our society changes, so do our notions of propriety. What was accepted etiquette 200 years ago would be considered absurd today. Nowhere is this more apparent than in the traditions and rituals surrounding weddings. If you have any doubts, you need only consult the history books.

In early Rome, it was considered proper etiquette to crumble pieces of wedding cake over the bride and groom's heads. Today, try crumbling a piece of frosting-covered wedding cake over a bride's elaborate coiffure and see just how much she appreciates it.

Or consider the medieval wedding feast, an occasion fraught with its own rules of etiquette. There was a correct way to do everything. The dishes had to be served in a specific order, and only so many fingers could be used to hold the meat for carving. Proper medieval etiquette required that the meat be cut with a knife and then eaten with the fingers. Try pulling that off at the next reception you attend.

The Victorians were required by etiquette and law to have weddings in the morning, usually followed by a wedding breakfast. Victorian men who married were expected to send calling cards to those acquaintances that he and his new bride wished to continue seeing after they married. In other words, all former relationships ended with the marriage unless the new husband sent his and his new wife's calling card to certain friends, giving them permission to call upon them as a married couple.

While these examples may seem extreme, it is important to note that even wedding etiquette, which was *de rigueur* fifty, or even thirty, years ago has gone the way of parasols and calling cards.

The focus of this book is on one aspect of wedding etiquette that has remained constant. While other wedding trends may come and go, the need to properly thank your wedding guests for their generosity will always remain. No matter what other traditions we decide to incorporate or discard, the two great cornerstones of etiquette — graciousness and appreciation — will never become extinct. Quite the opposite. Now more than ever, as society moves faster and harder and becomes more driven than at any time in the past, it is essential to maintain polite, gracious interaction — lest we all turn into cranky curmudgeons. By polite, I don't mean stilted and reserved. On the contrary, I mean warm, thoughtful and aware of the effect our actions have on each other.

Showering newlyweds with gifts as they begin their new life together is certainly a warm, thoughtful act of generosity on the part of gift givers. There are few other occasions in your adult life when you will be offered such bounty. In fact, there are perhaps only three: your wedding, when you have your first child, and when you celebrate one of your big anniversaries like the Silver 25th or the Golden 50th.

While this book is specifically written for the bride and groom who face the daunting task of writing an enormous quantity of thank you notes in a relatively short period of time, the principles apply to any occasion where you receive a gift.

Writing thank you notes does not have to be a tiresome chore. With the right attitude, the necessary tools and good organization, the task of thanking people for the gifts they have given you can become manageable and pleasant. (Yes, I said pleasant!)

This book is devoted to showing you how to do just that.

*All the fun's in how you say a thing.* — ROBERT FROST

# 1
# THANK YOU NOTE BASICS

*Everything You Need to Know about Thank You Note Etiquette*

WHETHER YOU RECEIVE thirty gifts or three hundred, the task of getting thank you notes out in the required amount of time can seem like a daunting challenge. It's tempting to convince yourself that if you've thanked the gift giver in person, then surely that should be enough.

It isn't.

It's also tempting to think of all the lovely mail merge capabilities on your word processing program or the multiple addressee function available with e-mail. Disregard those two thoughts because down that path lurks the impersonal, cookie-cutter-type thank you notes we all hope to avoid. It would not only be poor etiquette, but it would also come across as a half-hearted, cursory gesture at best.

In our weaker moments, it's easy to think of composing wedding thank you notes as a laborious chore. However, it is possible to turn this activity into a gracious ritual — one that allows us to focus on our friends and family for a few minutes each day during our busy schedules — especially since some of your favorite people will go out of their way to spend time, money and energy to ensure you have a wonderful start in your new life together. The very least you'll want to do is spend ten minutes of your time thinking about them and their gifts, and communicating how much their thoughtfulness means to you.

Now for the basics. Thank-you-note basics are deceptively simple and can be boiled down to three simple rules:

1.  Thank you notes *are* required.

2.  Thank you notes *need* be sent out in a timely manner.

3.  Thank you notes *must* be handwritten by the bride or groom.

(You may wish to show rule number three to your spouse-to-be if he needs written verification of this point.)

## Thank You Notes Are Required

The giving or showering of wedding presents has become such an automatic response in our society that it's easy to lose sight of the fact that, in reality, wedding gifts *are not* mandatory. No gesture of generosity is. Unfortunately, the reverse is not true. While the giving of gifts may be an option, the sending of thank you notes isn't. Thank you notes are mandatory.

Thank you notes need to be sent to anyone who gives you a gift. This includes gifts of time and assistance, so the members of your wedding party — bridesmaids, groomsmen, ushers, maid of honor, etc. — should receive a note. Typically, their contribution is so central to the success of the wedding that it's customary to give them a thank you gift, which will be discussed later in this book. Notes also need to be written to any service provider whose services you were happy with, such as organists, caterers, florists, musicians, etc. And don't forget to thank those who volunteered to provide a wedding task for you, like a family friend who helped plan the wedding, your mother's cousin who decorated the cake, or your Aunt Dorothy who did the flower arrangements.

Keep in mind that separate thank you notes must be sent for multiple gifts from the same person. If you are lucky enough to receive an engagement gift, a shower gift, and a wedding gift from a single person, then he or she deserves a separate note for each gift. Especially since the giving of those gifts will be spread out over a broad space of time and the gift giver is entitled to a timely response for each one.

If you receive one gift from a group of people, you only have to send one thank you note to thank the entire group.

## Thank You Notes Need to Be Sent Out in a Timely Manner

First, since it's one of the most critical points of etiquette, let's define "timely manner."

The couple-to-be should send out a thank you note within two weeks for a gift received *before* the wedding. It cannot be stressed strongly enough how critical it is to keep up with thank you notes for the presents you get before the big day. Staying on top of these notes is one of the most effective tools you have to not feeling overwhelmed. Of course, it varies greatly, but some couples receive up to half of their gifts before the wedding. This can be a make or break issue when trying to get your thank you notes out on time. If you have three hundred guests, and half of them send you gifts before the wedding, that's one hundred fifty thank you notes you can get out of the way beforehand. That reduces the number of notes owed after the wedding to one hundred fifty. Obviously, getting that amount of notes out in the required amount of time is much more manageable than three hundred. Don't fall behind!

Some experts claim that the bride has one month after returning from her honeymoon in which to send out thank yous for all the gifts given at the wedding. Other experts feel that three months is more reasonable. Somewhere between the two seems to be the best compromise. Certainly try to get the notes out within one month, if at all possible. This will be easier if you've planned a small wedding of one hundred fifty guests or less, or receive a large number of presents before the wedding. It's easy to feel as if this one-month requirement is more in line with thirty or forty years ago, when many brides returning from their honeymoons were faced with far fewer limitations on their time. While one month is a

*Actually, it's never too late to send a thank you. Embarrassing as it may be, a year later is better than never. I'm sure you'll agree that it's better to send a tardy note to Aunt Martha than to feel as though you need to avoid her at family gatherings because you still "owe her a thank you note." If you make it charming and gracious enough, she'll most likely forgive you. Try to avoid that awkwardness, however, and get those notes out within three months.*

noble goal to aim for, most brides return to full-time jobs where work has been piling up for two weeks while they were away on their honeymoons. Or perhaps they need to leave immediately on a business trip. In these cases, the one-month time frame can seem almost impossible and three months makes more sense.

*Different things work for different people. Here's a trick some couples use to help them stay motivated to write their thank you notes on time: Don't allow yourself to use a gift until you've sent the thank you note. This can be a powerful incentive! Especially if winter is coming and you really, really want to crawl in between those new flannel sheets.*

That being said, I do recommend that you prioritize your thank you note writing. Write notes to those guests that you know will be calling your mother or mother-in-law in exactly one month in order to complain (sometimes gleefully) that they have yet to receive a note. Distant relatives or friends of your parents whom you don't know well and don't see very often should also be at the top of your list.

Prioritizing your list of who to send to first does two things. It allows you to get notes out right away to those people who are most likely to see a late note as a breach of etiquette and it allows you to save the easiest for last.

Most experts agree that a couple has three months in which to reply with a thank you note for gifts received after the wedding.

**Gift Acknowledgment Cards**

If you have a wedding of four hundred or more guests, it will be nearly impossible to get thank you notes out in a timely manner. Some brides have such demanding work schedules they know they'll need every minute of their three-month time allotment. In such instances you may wish to consider gift acknowledgment cards. These are preprinted cards you buy when you place your order for wedding stationery. Basically they acknowledge the receipt of a gift. This keeps the gift giver from having to worry about whether or not the gift has arrived, but it is NEVER a substitute for a true thank you note, which you will write as soon as you can. You may need to order some of these preprinted cards with your maiden name on them, and an additional supply with your married name. The following examples illustrate a couple of ways in which you can handle gift acknowledgment cards.

*~*

*Lindsay Anne Wellington*
*Wishes to thankfully acknowledge*
*The receipt of your wedding gift*
*And will be sending you a personal note*
*of thanks at a later date.*

~

*Mr. and Mrs. Daniel A. Bergen*
*Gratefully acknowledge the receipt of your wedding gift.*
*A personal note of thanks will be sent at a later date.*

~

*Lindsay Anne Wellington and Stephen D. Cantrell*
*Wish to thankfully acknowledge*
*The receipt of your wedding gift*
*And will be sending you a personal note of thanks at a later date.*

 *The following people deserve thank you notes for their gifts of time and assistance.*

- ~ *Shower host or hostess*
- ~ *Usher*
- ~ *Maid of honor*
- ~ *Flower girl*
- ~ *Bride's parents*
- ~ *Anyone that contributed financially to the wedding*

- ~ *Bridesmaid*
- ~ *Groomsman*
- ~ *Best man*
- ~ *Ring bearer*
- ~ *Groom's parents*
- ~ *Vocalists*
- ~ *Musicians*

~ *Someone that said a special*       ~ *Minister*
  *prayer or read during*            ~ *Caterer*
  *the ceremony*                     ~ *Guest book attendant*
~ *Floral arranger*
~ *Friends or family that provide a wedding service*
  *(i.e., florals, catering, wedding planning) in lieu*
  *of a professional*

## Thank You Notes Must Be Handwritten
## By the Bride or Groom

When expressing your heartfelt gratitude for a particular gift, it's important that the recipient(s) of the thank you note be aware that you've taken some time and effort in letting them know how much you appreciate their thoughtfulness. It's also important to note that, increasingly, the groom is stepping in and sharing the responsibility of writing thank you notes. This seems especially appropriate when the gift comes from someone on his side of the family, his close friends, or a friend of his family that you've only met once or twice.

*When writing thank you notes for gifts received before the wedding, you need to use your maiden name. It's not acceptable to use your married name until after the wedding has taken place.*

The best recipe for writing successful heartfelt thank you notes is to combine the key ingredients of a form letter with a sprinkling of the sentiments found in a personal letter. While you want to be able to get through that stack of waiting thank yous relatively quickly (remember the one- to three-month guideline!), you also want each recipient to feel as if the note were written especially for her or him.

That's it. It's that simple.

*Every writer I know has trouble writing.* — JOSEPH HELLER

*I've never been big on the agony of writing.* — JAMES MICHENER

## Some Negative Things That May Need to Be Dealt With

### If a Gift Arrives Broken or Damaged.

Occasionally, through no fault of the gift giver, a gift will arrive broken or damaged. Unless the gift was sent insured, chances are the giver can do nothing about it at this point and would feel badly about the mishap — possibly even feel obligated to send a second gift — so avoid mentioning the fact that it's broken. If the gift was sent directly by a department store, you can contact the store directly. Their customer service department will most likely see to the replacement of the gift.

**If a Gift Needs to Be Returned.**

Even with the miracles of modern registry, duplicate gifts happen. You will no doubt receive three toasters, four can openers and six espresso machines. Don't feel as if you need to tell the gift giver that it was their particular toaster you returned. You can still say how thoughtful it was of them to send a toaster, because you and your husband always have two pieces of toast for breakfast and this will certainly speed up that process in the kitchen on those busy weekday mornings. They need never know that theirs was the one you returned. Do not send them a thank you note for whatever item you exchanged their original gift for.

**What Is It?**

There may be some gifts that will inspire you to say to your new husband, "What in the world is this?" In these instances, your thank you note will focus on the thought behind the gift rather than the gift itself. It's considered the height of impoliteness to say in a note, "Thank you for the lovely gift. Would you mind telling me what it is exactly?"

## The Card Gets Separated from the Gift and You Cannot Determine Who Gave It to You.

Occasionally, it happens. You're sitting on the floor, carefully opening one of the seventy-five gifts that surround you. You are being absolutely religious about jotting down the name of the gift giver and noting the gift on the back of the enclosed card or in a log. The phone rings. You jump up to answer it. When you come back you proceed to the next gift, forgetting that you hadn't finished jotting down all the information for the previous one. Or, you pick up a gift with no card on it. After searching through the piles, you still cannot find a lone card that might go with the gift.

This is the stuff thank-you-note nightmares are made of, and, unfortunately, there are no easy answers. Polite but discreet inquiries to your mother, or his, as to who may have given you the hand-held vacuum cleaner might turn up an answer. Or possibly not. If all else fails, you can try going through your invitation list and crossing off all the names of the people who you know have given you a present. It's possible that there will be only one name left. This would be most fortunate, and at this point you'll want to make a note about not answering the phone during the future writing of thank you notes.

**When the Wedding Is Called Off**

If the wedding is merely postponed for some reason, you must send an announcement to the guests letting them know of the postponement, but you may keep the gifts you've received.

When a wedding is called off or canceled, then all of the gifts need to be returned to their respective givers. This includes even the monogrammed and personalized ones. Send along a brief note with each gift you're returning, thanking the person for their thoughtfulness and explaining that the wedding will not be taking place. You are not required to give them a reason for the cancellation. When returning the gifts, the bride-to-be is responsible for writing to her friends and family as well as to those who are both friends of hers and the groom-to-be. The groom-to-be writes to his family and friends. The above procedure would also apply to weddings that are annulled soon after the ceremony.

# 2

# The Art of Writing Thank You Notes

*Writing, like life itself, is a voyage of discovery.* — Henry Miller

WHILE WRITING three hundred thank you notes can be about as inviting as a year's worth of past due homework, there are a few things to keep in mind.

1. Receiving the gifts certainly wasn't a chore! It was a joy. Try to recapture that sense of enthusiasm as you write your thank you notes.

2. In certain situations (and this is one of them), the only thing we are able to change is our own perspective.

3. With the right attitude, you really can turn the writing of these notes into a personally satisfying experience. (And not just because you crossed them off your to-do list!)

*Words are all we have.* — SAMUEL BECKETT

Since the first scribe put sharpened reed to soft clay and invented the first cuneiform, humankind has relied heavily on the written word for communicating and expressing itself. The writing of personal notes and letters is a beautiful art form that has almost been forgotten in today's world. A handwritten note attains a sense of permanence and personalization that cannot be captured with a preprinted greeting card, phone call, or an e-mail. (And it doesn't even need to be written on a clay tablet to do so!) It's a welcome bright spot in today's hi-tech society and should definitely not be relegated to the status of an outdated luxury.

In this universe dominated by technology, information and sound bytes, the old-fashioned practice of putting pen to paper can seem hopelessly slow and out of date. However, therein lies its charm. Let's face it, as much as most of us dread writing them, we all love to get letters. Short of refund checks from the IRS (or wedding gifts!) nothing else is quite as uplifting to find in your mailbox.

*If all of the above suggestions fail to lull you into the writing mood, put a bag of M & Ms on the desk in front of you and promise yourself two M & Ms for every note you finish!*

For women, this is especially true — perhaps because the fabric of our very lives consists of the connections we make with the people around us. As we thumb through the bills, catalogs, and junk mail we receive each day, our hearts leap slightly when we recognize the handwriting from someone who has taken the time to write a note. That extra bit of thoughtfulness means even more to us today than in the past. With faxes, modems, the Internet, DSL cable, cell phones and e-mail all working together to make personal correspondence a rarity, handwritten letters and notes are truly a welcome sight.

A written thank you has another often overlooked advantage. Sometimes we find it difficult to speak from our hearts. We feel awkward or embarrassed. We worry that the words might not sound right, or that we'll make the person we're speaking to feel uncomfortable. This is where putting our sentiments in a note has a huge advantage over saying them face to face. Like whispering secrets in the dark, expressing heartfelt thank yous on paper is often much easier than saying them out loud. This is *not* to suggest that you must turn every thank you note into a love letter or sappy bit of correspondence. But do permit yourself to admit to the person how much their gift touched you, or how meaningful it was to you that they traveled two hundred miles to attend your wedding. Remember that it is the sentiments you express, as much as the note itself, which will uplift the reader.

*You write by sitting down and writing. There is no particular time or place — suit yourself, your nature.* — BERNARD MALAMUD

## Setting the Mood

One of the most important tools at your disposal to help turn your note writing into a pleasant, relaxing ritual is where and how you do it. Here are some suggestions for making this a more personally satisfying experience.

Find a comfortable spot and transform it into a pleasant little nook for yourself. Whether you curl up on the sofa in front of a warm fire or on the chaise lounge in the backyard on a sunny afternoon, find a place that you like and make it special. Be sure to sit comfortably and spread out a bit if necessary.

Think of this time as a gift that you're giving to yourself as you correspond with your loved ones, and allow yourself the time to make those personal connections, which are so important in our lives.

~ Prepare a cup of hot tea or pour a glass of chilled wine to enjoy as your write your thank you notes.

~ Play some of your favorite music to lighten your mood and soothe your soul.

~ Place an aromatherapy candle nearby to help you relax. Take a few deep breaths and write from the heart.

*While this is certainly not required, some exceptionally conscientious brides and grooms have been known to write thank you notes on the plane to their honeymoon destination — especially if it's a long flight — with the joy of the wedding still fresh in their minds.*

*A man may write at any time, if he will set himself doggedly to it.* — SAMUEL JOHNSON

# 3
# TOOLS OF THE TRADE

THE STATIONERY and writing tools you select are another area where you can really make note writing more fun and creative. Watch out, though! If you make it too enjoyable you might find yourself turning into an avid correspondent!

As you sit down to write your thank you notes, you'll want to have everything you need at your fingertips in order to make the process as efficient as possible. Note cards, stationery, stamps, pens, address book, and your list of gifts received should be stored together so you don't have to spend precious minutes tracking down supplies when, instead, you could be writing a thank you note.

# Stationery

## Formal

As with all other aspects of your wedding and the planning process, your own personal style dictates what types of stationery supplies you will gravitate to. If you had a formal wedding, you might wish to stick with the traditional style of thank you notes known as informals. These can be ordered at the same time that you order your wedding invitations and stationery. Informals are 4" x 5" cards and would match your wedding stationery. They can have your name, your spouse's name, or both your names on the front. They can be printed, embossed, or engraved. Traditionally, colors include white and ivory with blue or black ink, but other color schemes are becoming increasingly popular. Ecru with slate gray or deep burgundy ink still attains a very formal look but is not quite as run-of-the-mill as black and blue.

*Printed* — Offset printing is the standard printing process where ink is laid down flat on the paper. It is the least expensive of the processes and offers a wide variety of ink colors and type styles.

*Embossed* — This is the process of having the letters and artwork raised on the paper but without ink.

*Engraved* — Engraved stationery is the most formal and traditional, but also the most expensive. This is an old process whereby the paper is pressed onto a metal plate, causing the letters to be slightly raised on the paper.

*Thermography* — This process fuses ink and powder together on the paper to create raised letters, which resemble engraving. Since plates don't have to be made and the process is quicker, thermography can be about half the price of true engraving.

When ordering printed informals for thank you notes, it's important to remember to order plenty of them with your maiden name, as you cannot use your married name until the day of your wedding. Since many couples receive up to half of their gifts prior to the wedding, it's critical to have an ample supply in your maiden name. Check with your stationer to decide how much of each you should order. The number of gifts you receive before your wedding will vary depending on your own situation and what part of the country you live in, but your stationer will be able to make a good recommendation.

*If you run out of informals with your maiden name just a week or two before the wedding, go ahead and write the thank you on the stationery with your married name. Just don't send it out until after the wedding has taken place.*

**Informal**

If your wedding style fell into the more popular categories of semi-formal and informal, there are many, many options available to you. Let your creativity flow accordingly. In fact, if you prefer, you can have different stationery for different note recipients. Certainly the notes to your family and closest friends can be much more lively and creative than the one you send to you husband's Aunt Martha who has never worn a pair of jeans in her life and still owns seventeen pairs of white gloves (and maybe even a parasol or two).

In selecting the materials you use, choose things that are pleasing to you. We are much more likely to use something that we enjoy, rather than something we don't. If you want to stick with a traditional single sheet of stationery folded over, there's no need to limit yourself to white and ivory. There are hundreds of choices of stationery sheets available today with unlimited colors, textures, prints and botanical elements. There should be no problem finding one or two, or a dozen, that will make writing thank you notes fun for you. It is perfectly acceptable to have a stationery wardrobe!

There are wonderful note cards in a similar array of styles and colors — some preprinted with the words Thank You, and others merely decorative on the outside. My only recommendation would be to steer clear of any note cards that have the thank you message itself already printed on the inside, as in the tradition of a greeting card. This is one time where you must find your own words.

## Writing Instruments

Similarly, with writing utensils, don't let yourself be limited to whatever pen happens to be lying next to the phone. The right pen can make writing a thoroughly amenable task or a tortured and ink-spotted one. The very way that the ink flows from the tip of the pen onto the paper can make writing a much more satisfying, tactile experience.

Many professional writers swear by a particular type of pen. I personally can never put pen to paper unless I'm using a Pilot v 7. Another writer I know suffers from the most tortured writer's block until he has his Uniball in hand. Others prefer the old-world elegance of a fountain pen, complete with different colors of bottled ink. Calligraphy pens, the inexpensive felt tipped ones, make any handwriting look instantly more formal and stylized. For a truly creative and whimsical thank you note, let yourself play with some of the fun "gel" ink-based pens, which are available in every color imaginable.

If you're a practical kind of note writer, then look to one of the ergonomically designed pens that are specifically designed to reduce writer's cramp and tired hands. If you have two hundred thank you notes to write, you'll be glad you did!

## Special Embellishments

Sealing wax has made a comeback in popularity. It comes in a nice selection of colors and in a wide variety of seals. Use an elegant symbol such as a fleur-de-lis, or your new initial. The metallic colors make wonderful eye-catching seals. If you love the look of wax seals but don't see yourself having the patience to light the wax, drip it, then impress it with your seal, you might want to check out the new wax seals on the market. They are adhesive-backed and sport the same elaborate look of the original wax but without all the fuss and muss.

And let's not forget stickers. Stickers are not just for kids. There are many elegant, works-of-art quality stickers out on the market today. If yours was an informal wedding, you can certainly explore this option for your thank you notes.

## Organize It!

Never underestimate the power of good organizational tools to make you feel in control of your life. All the supplies in the world won't do you a bit of good if you can't find them when you need them! Keep all your supplies in some type of organizer that will allow you to keep them together and handy.

Whether your taste runs to modern and functional or old-world romantic, there is an organizer out there for you. It could be an old-fashioned letter desk with a lift-up top, a utilitarian plastic storage tub, a briefcase, one of the jewel-toned accordion files from an office supply store, or a lovely antique-style hat box. Whatever brings you pleasure, but be sure to use something. And make sure it's convenient and pleasant to look at. Remember that this organizer is to become your constant companion for the next four to five months.

Your organizer should hold stationery, pens, stamps, address book, list of gifts received, pre-addressed envelopes, and any embellishments you might wish to use.

*Keep a second, smaller organizer available that will accommodate a small supply of thank you notes and other necessary items. You can carry it with you wherever you go. Then if you get stuck waiting for an appointment or have a few spare minutes during your lunch hour, you can easily jot off a note or two.*

# 4
# A Touch of Inspiration

*Special Touches and Unique Ideas for Your Thank You Notes*

F OR SOME THANK YOUS, words simply aren't enough. This chapter covers those situations where you may want to add a little something extra — or really go all out, whether you want your thank you note to stand out from the crowd, or you feel that the thank you demands more of a grand gesture than just a written note.

## A Picture Is Worth a Thousand Words

It used to be that the time factor in taking photographs and having them developed was too lengthy to consider including them with your thank you notes. Not so any more. The new advancements in film developing, from one-hour photo labs to digital cameras and pictures that you can print out on your own computer, reduce the time considerations to nil. Here are a few suggestions to get you thinking creatively.

~ Have double prints made from the disposable cameras you had placed around the tables at your wedding reception. If you have a photograph of the person or persons you are sending the thank you note to, include a snapshot of them enjoying the festivities. It will be a fun, visual reminder of the wedding.

~ Include a ceremonial photo of you and your spouse in the thank you note. Friends or relatives who couldn't be there in person will especially welcome this.

~ If you have an aunt who is an avid baker, or a friend who loves floral arranging, consider including a snapshot of your wedding cake or the truly stunning flower arrangement at your reception. You are likely to find a good shot taken from one of the disposable cameras.

~ A cute, candid shot of the ring bearer or flower girl is a nice way to say thank you to their parents.

~ Depending on the gift, you might consider taking a snapshot of it on display in your new home, or being used by you and your spouse. A picture of the cut crystal vase filled with a lovely bouquet would surely be appreciated by the gift giver, as would a photo of your husband grilling steaks on your new barbecue. These kinds of photos are fun to include in your thank you notes.

## Other Inspirations

~ A mere ribbon is so simple and yet it always makes such a wonderful impression. Tying dainty little ribbons around the letters and notes we write really does make them seem even more special. From the most dainty 1/16" pastel satin ribbons to the bolder, 1/2" sheer organza edged in gold, there is a ribbon out there that will complement your stationery style.

~ If not overdone, enclosing a few dried flower petals, a tiny sprig of dried rosemary or lavender, or other botanical adds a romantic element. If you promise yourself to use no more than five or six pieces, a festive wedding confetti (perhaps one you used at your wedding?) will add a nice surprise. The key here is not to overdo. No one appreciates an onslaught of confetti pouring from an envelope, making it necessary to get out the vacuum cleaner!

## For the Craft Enthusiast

If you're one of those people who love to spend your evenings and weekends making things, you might consider directing that talent to your thank you notes. It will make doing them much more fun, and make them a lot more special for the recipient.

Some crafts that lend themselves particularly well to note cards are:

*Stacked Paper Sculptures* — Cut or tear a variety of interesting papers and "stack" them in a paper "sculpture" stack. Textured papers, crinkled, metallic, matte, rice paper, all add interesting visual and tactile elements to the look. You can then top it all off with a bit of tied ribbon or interestingly shaped wire.

*Lace Doilies* — These lend themselves handily to note cards with a Victorian touch.

*Scrapbook Kits* — The different elements that are available for scrapbooks can also be adapted to fun, creative, thank you notes. Use the stencils, cut outs and other tools that come in these kits to make your thank yous one-of-a-kind.

*Embossing* — Many craft enthusiasts enjoy doing embossing work. If this is a hobby of yours, think how elegantly it will transfer itself to thank you cards.

*Rubber Stamping* — Rubber stamping has worked itself into an art form with all of the variety of rubber stamps, ink colors, and special effects available today. Again, let your imagination run wild as you create mini pieces of art to convey your thanks.

*Stenciling* — Stenciling is one of the easiest and simplest ways to enhance your thank-you-note cards. Again, the wide variety of stencil styles available on the market today just about ensure that you'll be able to find one to suit your own taste.

*Botanical Prints* — There are two different ways to go about this option. One is to use botanical elements — interesting leaves, flowers, flower petals, even cut fruit! — to "paint" or "stencil" the card. Another option, if you enjoy gardening and drying your florals, is to embellish the note cards with the dried flowers and leaves you have collected and pressed.

### Attendant Gifts

Traditionally, in order to thank wedding attendants for all their help and support, thank you gifts are given to them. For bridesmaids, these can be given at the bridesmaids' luncheon, or the rehearsal dinner. For the other attendants, the gifts are usually given at the rehearsal dinner. These gifts are meant to be lasting tokens of appreciation and to commemorate your wedding day. Gifts are most often given to:

~ Bridesmaids and Ushers

~ Honor Attendants

~ Ring bearer and Flower girl

~ Any non-professional who contributes to your wedding ceremony by way of reading, playing an instrument, or singing

~ Those who help at the reception by attending the guest book, handing out rice or birdseed, and so on

~ Parents

While these gifts don't need to be expensive, you do want them to convey an appropriate sense of importance for the support you've been given. Bridesmaids or women that you wish to thank for their contributions might enjoy any of the following items:

Jewelry box or jewelry, either to be worn at the wedding or for individual use

Gloves or handkerchiefs

Earrings, a locket or pearls

Small perfume bottle or atomizer

Picture frame

Sachet

Purse

Compact or makeup brushes

Vase

Stationery, business card holder or key ring

Scented candle or other aromatherapy products

Coffee mug with a variety of coffee beans or a charming teapot for the tea drinker

Gift certificate or a personally selected gift basket

Flower girl gifts can be similar to those given to the bridesmaids — either a miniature version or something similar but interpreted for a child.

For some reason, men often seem harder to shop for. Here are some ideas for your ushers, groomsmen and best man:

| | |
|---|---|
| Money clip | Pocket knife |
| Tie tack | Cuff links |
| Cigar case or cigar cutter | Necktie |
| Beer stein or Martini set | Key ring |
| Pocket flask | Wallet |

Gift certificate to a sports superstore or tickets to a sports event

A wonderful gift to thank your parents or his would be a beautifully framed photograph, a framed wedding invitation to commemorate the day, or some other personalized keepsake.

# 5
# MECHANICS

*Grammar is the grave of letters.* — ELBERT HUBBARD

WHILE IT IS IMPORTANT not to embarrass yourself (or your mother or fourth-grade grammar teacher), thank-you-note writing is one of the forms of writing where content and sentiment far outweigh the need to be entirely grammatically correct. Don't let yourself be frozen by Thank You Note Performance Anxiety. It's much more important for you to convey the true sentiment behind your words than it is to get each comma and semicolon exactly right. Remind yourself that these are friends and relatives who want to know that you received their gift and found it helpful or meaningful to you. An added sentence or two about how the two of you are doing now that the wedding festivities are over would be a welcome touch.

*If you're truly stuck for words, imagine yourself telephoning this person to express your thanks. Play out the conversation in your head (or aloud if no one else is nearby!), then quickly jot it down on a piece of scratch paper. Though it may need some polishing, you most likely have caught the "essence" of the note you will write.*

When writing thank you notes, it's best to compose your words in a warm conversational style, as if you were conversing with the person. You will want to imprint each note with your own personality and distinctly chosen words. In essence, write from the heart and it will be just fine.

An added bonus to the more conversational style is that it tends to be wordier than just plain writing. Since you want to make your thank you note appear somewhat substantial in nature, this subtlety works to your advantage. For example:

*Thank you for the flatware serving set* becomes *David and I want to especially thank you for the perfect flatware server set.*

*All morning I worked on the proof of one of my poems, and I took out a comma; in the afternoon, I put it back.* — OSCAR WILDE

## The Components of a Thank You Note

1.  Address the gift giver by name and include a salutation.

2.  Include the words "thank you" in your acknowledgment of the gift. Be sure to mention the gift by name and be very specific about it (and very, very correct.) It's also important to note in your acknowledgment *who* is thanking them. "John and I want to thank you for the lovely Persian rug."

3.  Say something nice about the gift, either how much you like it or what you plan to do with it.

4.  Add a short sentence or two with a personal message. This might pertain to how you're settling into your new house, life, or something about your honeymoon, or just mentioning how much you enjoyed seeing them at your wedding.

5.  Signature line.

6.  Optional: It's always a nice touch to have the spouse that didn't write the thank you note add a personal P.S. in his or her own handwriting.

## Other Note Writing Tips:

Always include a date, traditionally in the top left or right hand corner. If you are striving for an old-fashioned touch, you can date the note at the bottom.

Keep careful records of who gave what to you, and be careful not to let those unwritten thank you notes pile up.

Develop a note-writing system with your spouse that prioritizes your responsibilities: yours, his, ours, close friends, family, distant relations, etc.

Wedding thank yous should go out on a first-come, first-served basis. For gift givers who were unable to attend the wedding, it's a nice gesture to include a wedding or engagement photo.

Never mention the words *cash, check* or *money* in your thank you note. Instead, focus on the thought behind the gift. And never, ever mention the amount.

In the sections that follow, you will find samples of each of the elements that need to be included in a thank you note. Some will work for you, others won't. They are intended to give you an idea of how many different ways there are to say thank you, and to help eliminate the impression of having said the same thing too many times before.

Take the words and phrases and make them your own. Use the ones that sound the most natural coming from you. Don't use the more formal phrases if you always chat in a relaxed, casual manner. Conversely, don't use overly familiar phrasing that you normally wouldn't use in a spoken conversation. These ideas are meant to be jumping off points in helping you express the words and sentiments that are uniquely your own.

# 6
# SALUTATIONS

*W*HILE THE RECIPIENT of your letter will certainly dictate the tone and flavor of your thank you note, you will most likely begin all of them with "Dear". There are other salutations used in writing letters, but most are either too formal or too casual for wedding thank you notes. Certainly if you want to start a note to someone you are especially close to, "Dearest" is a nice change and suggests you are about to say something truly heartfelt. Depending on your relationship to the receiver, here are a few other suggestions for ways to begin your personal note:

> Greetings!
> Hi there!
> My dear Sam,
> We're back!

Darling Yvonne,

Dearest Friends,

To a Favorite Niece,

This is where it will come in handy to have saved, or duly recorded, your guest list names and how you addressed them. While Mr. and Mrs. Randall Worthington is perfectly correct on the envelope, you will want to start your letter with Dear Randall and Sharon.

The same rules for addressing your wedding invitations apply to your thank you notes. Women are addressed as Mrs., Ms., Miss, or their professional title. Mr. works for all men unless they have a professional title that they prefer to use. The husband's first and last names (i.e., Mr. and Mrs. Nelson Clark) have traditionally been used to address a married couple. However, as more and more women keep their maiden names, or acquire professional titles, this is changing somewhat. It is not uncommon to address correspondence to Mr. John Cunningham and Ms. Marion Vanden, or to Mr. Lewis Smith and Dr. Jane White.

# 7
# THANK YOU NOTE THESAURUS

*A writer lives in awe of words for they can be cruel or kind,*
*and they can change their meanings right in front of you.*
*They pick up odors and flavors like butter in a refrigerator.*
— JOHN STEINBECK

WHEN WRITING a number of notes in a row, it's very easy to feel as if they all sound the same or you are being boring and unoriginal. This section is to help you in finding overlooked words as you try and describe your enthusiasm to the gift giver.

Instead of *really* or *very*, how about:

| | |
|---|---|
| Wonderfully | Exceptionally |
| Positively | Uncommonly |

| | |
|---|---|
| Especially | Certainly |
| Rarely | Unusually |
| Largely | Greatly |
| Exceedingly | Intensely |
| Truly | Completely |

The following words make excellent substitutes for *pretty*:

| | |
|---|---|
| Beautiful | Elegant |
| Graceful | Exquisite |
| Superb | Handsome |
| Serene | Lovely |
| Radiant | Comely |
| Attractive | Gorgeous |

*Nice* is such a non-descriptive word. How about:

| | |
|---|---|
| Pleasant | Fine |
| Superior quality | Good |
| Admirable | Inviting |
| Wonderful | Thoughtful |
| Agreeable | Delightful |
| Careful | Considerate |

Excellent            Refined

Right                Accurate

Delicate             Exact

Particular           Subtle

# 8

# PERSONALIZED PHRASES

*Writing is just having a sheet of paper, a pen, and not a shadow of an idea of what you're going to say.* — FRANÇOISE SAGAN

IN ORDER TO AVOID what I call the three-sentence wonder, here are some examples of gracious and personalized comments you can include in your thank you note to show that you've put some time and energy into the process.

## Regarding the Wedding

- ~ We so enjoyed seeing you at our wedding.
- ~ It was extraordinarily thoughtful of you to come all that way for our wedding.

- Our wedding day would not have seemed complete if you hadn't been there.

- One of the most treasured memories of our wedding day is seeing all of our favorite people gathered together in one room.

- Having you at our wedding made it just that much more special.

- Weddings are meant to be shared and we are so glad you could be there to share ours.

- Unfortunately, we didn't get to spend as much time with each of our guests as we would have liked. It must be an occupational hazard when you're a bride and groom!

- Even though I was unable to spend as much time with you as I would have liked, knowing you were there was hugely important to me.

- Can't wait to see you at the wedding!

- I was quite relieved to hear you can make it to our wedding. It just wouldn't be the same without you there.

- I'm terribly excited about seeing you again. We have all sorts of fun things planned for the weekend, so you'd better rest up.

∾ We are really glad you'll be able to make it to the wedding and look forward to seeing you there.

∾ We're thrilled you're coming to the wedding. I can't wait to see you again!

∾ I'm so sorry you won't be able to make it to the wedding, but both John and I certainly understand.

∾ While we're disappointed you can't make it to the wedding, it's comforting to know your thoughts and good wishes are with us.

∾ I'm so sorry you'll be out of town that weekend. Jim has told me lots of wonderful things about you and I had been looking forward to meeting you. Let's catch up after we return from our honeymoon.

**Mentioning Your Recent Honeymoon**

These phrases can be rewritten to reflect where you spent your own honeymoon. There are many different ways to convey the same sentiment so that it still seems fresh and original.

∾ We had so much fun on our honeymoon! I didn't realize how much we needed the R & R after planning the wedding.

~ We ran into some unseasonable weather on our honeymoon, but it didn't really matter. It just felt good to relax and unwind together.

~ The Hawaiian sunsets stole our breath away!

~ The Caribbean sunsets were truly breathtaking.

~ The sunsets in Bermuda, with their blues and golds and pinks, were incredible.

~ The sunsets in the islands are a memory that will last us a lifetime.

~ The tranquility of the pink sand beaches and crystal blue waters provided a much-needed calm after all the pre-wedding activities.

~ The relaxed pace of Mexico's sunny, friendly beaches were a perfect way to recuperate from the entire frenzy of planning the wedding.

~ The warmth and friendliness of Cabo San Lucas made it the perfect place to relax after our wedding.

~ Puerto Vallarta was charming and we spent a very peaceful and relaxing week lounging on the white sand beaches.

~ Acapulco was so much fun! Lots of things to see and do with never a dull moment. I think we may need a week to recover!

~ Wouldn't you just know it! A tropical storm moved in the day after we arrived in Hawaii and it was still raining when we left. Luckily, the resort where we stayed was fabulous, and we managed to have a wonderful time in spite of the weather.

~ In Maui, both Paul and I were able to try snorkeling for the first time. It was incredible to see all the colorful tropical fish swimming right under our noses!

~ The island of Kauai was so lush and green! A true tropical paradise and a perfect place to spend our honeymoon.

~ Let us tell you, there is nothing like touring Napa Valley from a hot air balloon to really put everything in perspective!

~ The people of Tahiti were so warm and friendly, and finally I was able to make good use of my high school French.

~ The fresh pineapple in Moorea was unbelievable. If I could, I would have snuck a dozen of them back with me in my suitcase.

~ Our hotel was right on the edge of a lagoon and ever so peaceful!

~ We tried to paddle in a traditional canoe, but Jay managed to tip us over in the first three minutes. Luckily the water was warm and clear so it didn't matter.

- The nightlife was fabulous! We danced and partied to our hearts content.

- I couldn't believe it! Two days into our honeymoon I came down with a horrible case of the stomach flu. The only good part about it was that Stephen proved himself to be a wonderful, thoughtful nurse!

- We loved Hawaii! We want to go back every year for the rest of our lives!

- It's amazing how quickly the hustle and bustle of everyday life falls away under the serenity of the Bahamas.

- We discovered a fabulous new recipe for seafood enchiladas on our honeymoon, and I can't wait to try them out on you when we get back.

# 9
# GIFT SPECIFIC PHRASES

*S*INCE FINDING the right words can be so difficult, here are some "gift specific" phrases that might be of help.

## Formal China

~ Thank you so much for the place setting of our formal china. We searched and searched until we found the perfect style we could both agree on.

~ We plan to entertain a lot for our work and the formal place setting you gave us will certainly help create a sophisticated, refined atmosphere.

~ Steve and I want to thank you for the place setting of our formal china. It rounds out our set to twelve place settings. I guess that means we'll be having Thanksgiving dinner here this year!

## Serving Dishes

~ The serving pieces you gave us round out our china set perfectly. I suspect they're the kinds of things one always covets but never quite gets around to buying for oneself, so I'm thrilled to receive them.

~ The ceramic lasagna pan is just perfect, as lasagna is one of my favorite foods and one of the few things I know how to cook! It's also great for feeding a crowd — so as soon as we get settled, we'll set something up and have you over for dinner.

~ The quiche dish is charming! I've always made do with a pie plate, but this will work much better — and recently I found a quick recipe for quiche that Thomas will actually eat. (Quiche Lorraine — it's the bacon and Swiss cheese he couldn't resist — with none of those yucky vegetables normally found in quiches.)

~ Bradley and I were delighted to receive such a striking serving platter. The design is uniquely fresh and modern, and it will work for just about all occasions.

~ Thank you so much for the salad bowl set. Salads are an absolute staple in my diet and they'll look tremendously attractive in this beautiful set.

~ It's surprising how the right salt and pepper shakers can really make or break the look of a table. These that you have sent us are magnificently carved, yet so functional. And with Mark being a pepper addict, they surely will get lots of use.

## Candlesticks

~ The crystal candlesticks are truly exquisite in their workmanship and will add some much-needed panache to our décor!

~ The silver candelabra is so elegant, truly a keepsake heirloom that we will want to hand down to our own children. It occupies a place of honor in our dining room.

## Example of a Letter Expressing Thanks

*Dear Aunt Agatha,*

*Glenn and I want to thank you so much for the elegant silver candlesticks! They add a wonderful, stately touch to our dining room and remind me of the wonderful Thanksgiving dinners we used to have around your dining room table.*

*I'm sorry you weren't feeling well enough to make it to the wedding. I've enclosed a snapshot or two of the reception, which I thought you might enjoy seeing. I'll be traveling your way on business next month and am hoping we can arrange a quick visit. I'll bring the wedding pictures!*

*In the meantime, thank you again for the generous gift. We will treasure it deeply, as it is sure to become one of our own family's heirlooms.*

*Fondly,*
*Delia and Glenn*

**Serving Tray**

*Dear Uncle Max and Aunt Irene,*

*Kevin and I can't thank you enough for the beautiful wooden serving tray. The hand-painted flowers are so intricate and real looking — it's like having a small garden inside! We will use it often, I'm sure, both for entertaining and when I manage to talk Kevin into serving me breakfast in bed!*

*It was absolutely wonderful seeing you two at the wedding. You cut quite the figure on the dance floor. Kevin and I can only hope to have half as much fun together when we reach your age.*

*With love and good memories,*
*Dana and Kevin*

## Soup Tureen

*Dear Mr. and Mrs. Robertson,*

*David and I just love the soup tureen you gave us for a wedding present and wanted to extend our sincerest appreciation. It was a lovely, thoughtful gift and will add an elegant touch to our dinner table.*

*It was wonderful to see you at the wedding. I hadn't realized that it had been so long since the last time we saw each other. Again, thank you for the most thoughtful gift.*

*Sincerely,*

*David and Kelley Balch*

**Coffee Maker**

*Rick and I want to thank you so much for the coffee maker. The electronic timer feature is especially great since we are now waking up to coffee already brewed and ready to pour!*

~

*Tim and I were thrilled to receive the espresso machine! As you know, I'm a confirmed latte addict and I'm afraid I've got Tim hooked now as well. We've already agreed that, since he gets up earlier than I do during the week, he'll serve me latte in bed and I'll do the same for him on the weekends. What a great way to start married life — latte in bed!*

**Fondue Set**

*David and I were so excited to receive the fondue set you sent us for a wedding gift! I've only had fondue twice in my life, but thoroughly enjoyed it each time. David is already putting together his first Super Bowl Party and we're planning on using it then.*

**Cookware**

*I love the nonstick idea of the roaster you sent us. Since I know next to nothing about cooking, I need all the help I can get! It'll sure make things easier.*

❀

*Both John and I love to cook, so we'll be getting tons of enjoyment out of the stainless steel pots and pans you sent.*

❀

*I've promised myself I'd learn how to cook this year, and these state-of-the-art pans will be a wonderful incentive.*

❀

*Your reputation as a cook is legendary in Ted's family. I'm sure that this cookware you've chosen for us will help me with my own cooking skills.*

**Vases**

*We are simply enchanted with the set of delicate crystal bud vases. They are truly charming and make me smile every time I look at them.*

❀

*You know how much I adore flowers. Now I have a perfect excuse to indulge my passion.*


## Example of a Letter Expressing Thanks

*Dear Caroline,*

*Mark and I want to let you know just how much we adore the exquisite cut crystal vase you gave us for our wedding present. It is truly breathtaking in the way it catches and reflects the light. Even the most humble of wildflowers will look stunning in this vase. It holds a place of honor in our living room and, of course, we'll think of you every time we look at it.*

*Caroline, I can't tell you how much I loved having you at the wedding. Your bubbling personality always makes every occasion seem brighter.*

*Thanks again,*
*Tracy and Mark*

## Kitchen Appliances

*Dear Aunt Helen and Uncle Fred,*

*Bill and I were thrilled to receive the bread machine that you sent us for a wedding present. Every night when Bill comes home from work he goes over to it and hovers hopefully! I've promised him we will try it this weekend. He says he's never had homemade bread, and I know I haven't had any since the last time I ate at your house.*

*While I'm very sorry you couldn't make it out for the wedding, it was nice to know that your thoughts and good wishes were with us. Once again, thank you for the super gift. It's definitely something we'll both enjoy.*

*With much love,*
*Bill and Vicky*

*Dear Joe,*

    *Natalie and I want to thank you for the popcorn maker. As you already know, I'm addicted to the stuff so we'll be using it regularly.*

    *It was good to see you and Jan at the wedding. And you were right about Maui — the snorkeling was awesome! Natalie even gave it a try and she had a blast, too.*

    *Thanks again for the popcorn maker. In fact, I might just make a bowl of it right now to help me get through the next ten thank you notes I have to write!*

                *Yours,*

                *Dan and Natalie*

*Dear Jennifer,*

*Donald and I would like to thank you very much for the pasta maker. Pasta is absolutely one of our favorite dishes — in all its forms — so we're confident we'll get lots and lots of use out of it. In fact, as soon as we get unpacked, (if we ever get unpacked!) it will be one of the first things we use. I'm looking forward to the sight of drying strands of pasta hanging from ceiling to floor. It will make me feel like such a professional cook!*

*Our new apartment is charming and I can't wait for you to see it. It's in a newly renovated part of town and within walking distance of almost all of my favorite shops. Next time you come for a visit, I'll have to show you the sights.*

*Thanks again for the wonderful gift.*

*Love and take care,*

*Elizabeth and Donald*

## Crystal Decanter

*Dear Uncle Ralph,*

*Thad and I want to let you know how much we appreciate the cut crystal decanter set you sent us for a wedding present. It is just perfect in its old-world style and elegance, and we can't thank you enough. I'm sure all our guests will enjoy it as much as we do.*

*Our honeymoon was wonderful! Our hotel was right on the edge of a lagoon and so peaceful. Just what we needed.*

*Once again, thank you for the exquisite gift.*

*Love,*

*Denise and Thad*

## Bedding

*Steve and I want to thank you for the flannel sheet set. They are absolutely fabulous. I don't think I've ever slept as warm and cozily as I do under those sheets — or maybe it's Steve. Hard to tell.*

～

*Thank you for the much needed sheet set. The crisp, clean pattern is so elegant! It will truly make our bedroom seem special.*

∾

*Jim and I want to thank you for the down comforter. It's such a lightweight way to stay warm at night! I'm sure it will last us for many, many years to come.*

∾

*The electric blanket you got us is just perfect! Especially the dual controls. Doug and I never seem to be the same temperature — he's an inferno and I'm closer to a Popsicle. This is the perfect answer.*

∾

*Lawrence and I want to thank you for the beautiful bedroom accessories. I've always wanted the luxury of a bed ruffle and shams, but never quite got around to making it happen. They are truly lovely, and the warm floral pattern makes our bedroom a light and cheery haven!*

## Bath Towels and Accessories

Brian and I can't thank you enough for the luxurious bath towels. They are so thick and plush that it makes drying off a truly indulgent experience!

~

Jay and I would like to thank you for the gorgeous bath towels you gave us for our wedding. The color is just perfect and really livens up an otherwise unexceptional bathroom.

~

Thanks for the great bath mat. Its thick warmth is a great alternative to cold tile first thing in the morning. It makes our toes very happy!

~

Thanks so much for the bathroom accessories. They look really cheerful sitting on our counter, and they certainly help to keep the bathroom more organized.

**Barbecue**

Todd and I want to thank you for the wonderful barbecue set. Todd is determined to learn the art of grilling and the tools will help a lot.

~

Todd and I want to thank all of you for the barbecue. It was such a generous gift, and I know we'll get lots of use out of it. Todd has been wanting to learn how to grill and I'm all for anything that encourages him to take turns with the cooking.

~

Todd and I want to thank you for the incredible barbecue you gave us for our wedding present. We can't wait until the weather gets nice enough so we can use it.

**Monetary Gift**

*Dear Mr. and Mrs. Henderson,*

*Justin and I want to thank you very much for your generous wedding gift. It will go toward buying a new comfy couch for our apartment. In fact, we already have a lovely one picked out — one that we plan to keep for many, many years.*

*We enjoyed seeing you at the wedding and only wish that there had been more time for visiting. Once again, thank you for your generous gift. We are extremely appreciative.*

*Sincerely yours,*

*Melanie and Justin*

*Dear Uncle Bob and Aunt Dora,*

*Thank you for the incredibly generous wedding gift. Rick and I were stunned and amazed — and very grateful. In fact, we already know exactly what we'll be using it for. The commute that Rick will be making from our new apartment is twice the distance as before, so we've been talking about getting a car that has better fuel economy. Your gift will go a long way toward making that happen. Thank you so, so much! Rick and I are truly awed by your generosity.*

*We've all been talking about how much fun it will be to see you when you come out for the wedding. Mom's already resting up for those late night chat sessions we always enjoy. Can't wait to see you!*

> *Love and kisses,*
> *Chrisy and Rick*

*Dear Jim and Vera,*

*Matt and I want to thank you for the very generous donation you made to our Honeymoon Registry. It will go a long way toward getting us there! We are so looking forward to the trip. The peace and quiet of an island getaway sounds ideal after all this wedding planning!*

*I'm sorry we won't be seeing you at the wedding, but I certainly understand what a long trip it is for you. Thank you again for your generosity.*

*Fondly,*

*Emily and Matt*

## Unusual or Unidentifiable Gifts

*Your gift was an original and clever idea.*

~

*We both appreciate the time and effort you must have spent finding such an original gift.*

~

Your gift to us will be a great conversation piece when we entertain.

~

Both Jay and I enjoy owning such a unique piece. It makes such a wonderful personal statement.

~

Neither of us has ever seen such an extraordinary piece before, but we already agree it will be very useful.

# *10*
# CLOSINGS

THERE ARE MANY OPTIONS to choose from and, again, your relationship with the note recipient will dictate your choice. "Sincerely" is certainly appropriate in all cases, but perhaps you wish to be a little more formal. In that case you might try Yours truly, Very truly yours, Respectfully yours, or Very cordially yours. Other less formal choices might include:

Very fondly,

Sincerely,

Love,

Sincerely yours,

Best wishes,

Cordially,

Regards,

Best regards,

Kindest regards,

With deepest appreciation,

Hugs and kisses,

With our most sincere appreciation,

Fondly,

Warm regards,

Affectionately,

As ever,

Love always,

With warmest affection,

Gratefully yours,

All the best,

When writing thank you notes before your wedding, you need to sign your maiden name. After the wedding, use whatever name you have chosen to use.

# 11
# SAMPLE THANK YOU NOTES

*For a Particular Event or Service*

**Throwing a Shower**

> *Dear Katy,*
>
> *Thank you so much for throwing such a spectacular shower. Everything was just incredible — the food, the flowers and decorations — you even managed to find games that were fun! I'm very touched by the amount of time and energy you put into this event, as well as everyone's generosity.*

*Once again, thanks for such an incredible afternoon. It will be one of my best wedding memories for years to come!*
*With warmest affection,*
*Molly*

~

*Dear Lila and Edward,*

*Jack and I want to thank you so much for the shower you had for us. Neither of us had been to a co-ed shower before and it was great fun. Jack especially enjoyed the evening, as he has never attended any kind of shower.*

*It was a fabulous time. The food and music were great and we cannot believe how many wonderful gifts we received. Thanks so much for hosting it.*
*With our most sincere appreciation,*
*Yvonne and Jack*

**An Engagement Party**

Dear Tanya,

Tim and I thank you from the bottom of our hearts for holding such an elegant engagement party in our honor. We had a great time and it was such a wonderful feeling to know that everyone was so thrilled about our engagement.

As usual, you were an exquisite hostess, serving the best food and drinks around — and somehow managing to see to it that everyone had a fabulous time. What a great way to start off our new life together!

As ever,

Margie and Tim

## Overseeing the Guest Book

*Dear Megan,*

*Thank you so much for offering to oversee the signing of the guest book. With so many details to see to on the Big Day, it was reassuring to know that you were taking care of this for us. I know Bill and I will treasure the guest book as a wonderful reminder of how many close friends and family celebrated our wedding with us. Thanks for making sure they all signed in!*

*Best regards,*
*Karen*

**Playing Music**

*Dear Claire,*

*Kirk and I want to thank you so much for providing such exquisite harp music at our wedding. Truly, no one makes those strings sing as sweetly as you do. The pieces you played were especially moving, and I can think of no better accompaniment to our marriage vows than you and your harp.*

*Thanks again for adding such a special, personal touch to our wedding ceremony. We're forever grateful to you*

*Sincerely,*

*Dorothy and Kirk*

## Handling the Floral Arrangements

*Dear Aunt Dorothy,*

*Luis and I want to thank you so much for taking on the huge task of doing the floral arrangements for our wedding ceremony and reception. They were truly exquisite and I'm still hearing comments from people as to just how magical they looked. You've always had a green thumb, but never have I appreciated it more than now.*

*Thanks again for putting so much effort into making our wedding day truly spectacular.*

*With much love,*

*Patti and Luis*

**Creating the Wedding Cake**

*Dear Sophia,*

*All I can say is Wow! I never knew you harbored such artistic talents, especially in a medium as challenging as frosting! Our wedding cake was definitely the showpiece of the reception. Everyone stopped to admire it. You truly outdid yourself and did a magnificent job. I can only imagine the hours and hours of work you must have put into it!*

*Thanks so much for offering to make our wedding cake. The results were incredible and Tom and I feel very lucky to have had such a personalized cake.*

*Affectionately,*
*Laurie and Tom*

## Being a Bridesmaid

*Dearest Patti,*

*I need to tell you how meaningful it was to have you as one of my bridesmaids. Sometimes, even with the closest of friends, it's hard to find the words to express exactly how I feel. Knowing you were there with Martin and me, and knowing how much we've shared together over the years made the moment so much more complete.*

*Your help and support over the last few chaotic months have been invaluable. I want to thank you for everything you've done — from helping to keep the other bridesmaids organized to just being there when I needed to talk. Your contribution to this wedding and its success has been enormous.*

*Thanks so much, Patti, for everything.*

*Love,*

*Christine*

## Acting as Usher/Groomsman

*Dear Josh,*

*I don't know why you were so nervous! Nancy and I thought you did a great job as an usher and we want to thank you for doing that for us. Nancy's Aunt Judith still talks about "that handsome young friend of yours." Have to admit, buddy, I'd never seen you in a tux before. Might not have recognized you on the street!*

*Seriously, I want to thank you for doing this for me. It's great to have friends you can count on.*

*Sincerely,*

*Zack*

**Canceling the Wedding**

*Dear Mr. and Mrs. Rothman,*

*Stephen and I have come to a mutual agreement to end our engagement. As difficult as it is to cancel the wedding, which seems to have taken on a life of its own, we both feel hugely relieved that we've made this decision now as opposed to after the wedding took place.*

*The tablecloth and placemats you selected for us are truly charming, but I'm sure you'll understand why I feel I need to return them to you. Thanks so much for your generosity and understanding.*

*Best regards,*

*Amanda*

## 12
# PUTTING IT ALL TOGETHER

OW YOU KNOW exactly what to do to tackle this somewhat daunting task before you — and with just the right attitude to make all your thank you notes come from the heart. This chapter, a step-by-step timeline, if you will, is going to show you how to combine all the elements we've talked about into a simple, easy-to-follow process that will allow you to manage your thank-you-note writing effectively.

1.  Order or purchase your stationery supplies. You may wish to do this when you order your wedding invitations, especially if you're going to be using informals or other printed or embossed stationery. Keep in mind, however,

that gifts can begin arriving as soon as the engagement is announced, so you might want to have something long before you've had a chance to confirm all the details that will need to go on your invitation.

2. If ordering preprinted stationery, make sure to order some in both your maiden name and the name you intend to use after the wedding.

3. Set up an attractive writing space.

4. Keep careful track of who sent what to you. As soon as a gift arrives, jot down the name of the giver and exactly what the gift was on the back of the card enclosed. Or better yet, note it in the log in the back of this book. Use an index card system. Whatever works. Just keep track.

5. Send thank you notes for gifts received prior to the wedding within two weeks of receipt. The sooner the better, and they really should be on a first-come, first-served basis.

6. Make sure each note thanks the giver, mentions the gift by name, and says how you'll use it or how much you enjoy it. Add a personal line or two at the end.

7. Keep all of your supplies in a handy organizer.

8.  As you address your wedding invitations, address your thank you notes at the same time.

9.  As you open all the gifts received at the wedding or when you return from your honeymoon, keep meticulous track of names and gifts. Avoid the embarrassment of not knowing who gave what.

10. Make up a list of "Thank You Note Triage", prioritizing the thank you notes you need to write.

11. Enlist your husband's help, especially for gifts received by his family members, or from friends of his family that you barely know.

12. Pace yourself, write a few thank you notes every day.

13. Reward yourself for a job well done.

## In Closing

*Dear Reader,*

*Thank you so much for taking the time to read this book. I'm hoping you found lots of tips and suggestions that turned your thank-you-note writing experience into a pleasant one.*

*One of the most important things to keep in mind is that weddings and wedding styles are as unique and different as the brides who plan them. Infuse your notes, like your wedding, with your own unique personal style. Some of the suggestions presented in this book will work for you, others will not. Please pick and choose those ideas, thoughts and advice that work best for you and ignore the others except for the Big Three : Thank you notes MUST be written for every gift, Thank you notes MUST be handwritten by the bride or groom, and Thank you notes MUST be written in a timely manner. Keep in mind that just because your best friend sat down and made handcrafted thank you notes, doesn't mean you have to as well. Just because your sister was so meticulous that she wrote her thank you notes on the plane to her honeymoon, doesn't mean that it's required. Invent a process that works best for you.*

*Once again, thank you for caring enough about the notes you write to consult this book. I wish you and your loved ones a long, wonderful life together filled with lots of occasions for heartfelt thank yous.*

*Sincerely,*
*Beverly Clark*

# INDEX

## *Gifts Received / Thank You Notes Sent*

| Date | Who Gave the Gift | Description of Gift | Thank You Note Due | Sent |
|------|-------------------|---------------------|--------------------|------|
|      |                   |                     |                    |      |
|      |                   |                     |                    |      |
|      |                   |                     |                    |      |
|      |                   |                     |                    |      |
|      |                   |                     |                    |      |
|      |                   |                     |                    |      |
|      |                   |                     |                    |      |
|      |                   |                     |                    |      |
|      |                   |                     |                    |      |

## Gifts Received / Thank You Notes Sent

| Date | Who Gave the Gift | Description of Gift | Thank You Note Due | Sent |
|------|-------------------|---------------------|--------------------|------|
|      |                   |                     |                    |      |
|      |                   |                     |                    |      |
|      |                   |                     |                    |      |
|      |                   |                     |                    |      |
|      |                   |                     |                    |      |
|      |                   |                     |                    |      |
|      |                   |                     |                    |      |
|      |                   |                     |                    |      |
|      |                   |                     |                    |      |

## Gifts Received / Thank You Notes Sent

| Date | Who Gave the Gift | Description of Gift | Thank You Note Due | Sent |
|------|-------------------|---------------------|--------------------|------|
|      |                   |                     |                    |      |
|      |                   |                     |                    |      |
|      |                   |                     |                    |      |
|      |                   |                     |                    |      |
|      |                   |                     |                    |      |
|      |                   |                     |                    |      |
|      |                   |                     |                    |      |
|      |                   |                     |                    |      |
|      |                   |                     |                    |      |

## *Gifts Received / Thank You Notes Sent*

| Date | Who Gave the Gift | Description of Gift | Thank You Note Due | Sent |
|------|-------------------|---------------------|--------------------|------|
|      |                   |                     |                    |      |
|      |                   |                     |                    |      |
|      |                   |                     |                    |      |
|      |                   |                     |                    |      |
|      |                   |                     |                    |      |
|      |                   |                     |                    |      |
|      |                   |                     |                    |      |
|      |                   |                     |                    |      |
|      |                   |                     |                    |      |

## *Gifts Received / Thank You Notes Sent*

| Date | Who Gave the Gift | Description of Gift | Thank You Note Due | Sent |
|------|-------------------|---------------------|--------------------|------|
|      |                   |                     |                    |      |
|      |                   |                     |                    |      |
|      |                   |                     |                    |      |
|      |                   |                     |                    |      |
|      |                   |                     |                    |      |
|      |                   |                     |                    |      |
|      |                   |                     |                    |      |
|      |                   |                     |                    |      |
|      |                   |                     |                    |      |

## Gifts Received / Thank You Notes Sent

| Date | Who Gave the Gift | Description of Gift | Thank You Note Due | Sent |
|------|-------------------|---------------------|--------------------|------|
|      |                   |                     |                    |      |
|      |                   |                     |                    |      |
|      |                   |                     |                    |      |
|      |                   |                     |                    |      |
|      |                   |                     |                    |      |
|      |                   |                     |                    |      |
|      |                   |                     |                    |      |
|      |                   |                     |                    |      |
|      |                   |                     |                    |      |

## Gifts Received / Thank You Notes Sent

| Date | Who Gave the Gift | Description of Gift | Thank You Note Due | Sent |
|------|-------------------|---------------------|--------------------|------|
|      |                   |                     |                    |      |
|      |                   |                     |                    |      |
|      |                   |                     |                    |      |
|      |                   |                     |                    |      |
|      |                   |                     |                    |      |
|      |                   |                     |                    |      |
|      |                   |                     |                    |      |
|      |                   |                     |                    |      |
|      |                   |                     |                    |      |

## Gifts Received / Thank You Notes Sent

| Date | Who Gave the Gift | Description of Gift | Thank You Note Due | Sent |
|------|-------------------|---------------------|--------------------|------|
|      |                   |                     |                    |      |
|      |                   |                     |                    |      |
|      |                   |                     |                    |      |
|      |                   |                     |                    |      |
|      |                   |                     |                    |      |
|      |                   |                     |                    |      |
|      |                   |                     |                    |      |
|      |                   |                     |                    |      |
|      |                   |                     |                    |      |

## Gifts Received / Thank You Notes Sent

| Date | Who Gave the Gift | Description of Gift | Thank You Note Due | Sent |
|------|-------------------|---------------------|--------------------|------|
|      |                   |                     |                    |      |
|      |                   |                     |                    |      |
|      |                   |                     |                    |      |
|      |                   |                     |                    |      |
|      |                   |                     |                    |      |
|      |                   |                     |                    |      |
|      |                   |                     |                    |      |
|      |                   |                     |                    |      |
|      |                   |                     |                    |      |

## *Gifts Received / Thank You Notes Sent*

| Date | Who Gave the Gift | Description of Gift | Thank You Note Due | Sent |
|------|-------------------|---------------------|--------------------|------|
|      |                   |                     |                    |      |
|      |                   |                     |                    |      |
|      |                   |                     |                    |      |
|      |                   |                     |                    |      |
|      |                   |                     |                    |      |
|      |                   |                     |                    |      |
|      |                   |                     |                    |      |
|      |                   |                     |                    |      |
|      |                   |                     |                    |      |

## Gifts Received / Thank You Notes Sent

| Date | Who Gave the Gift | Description of Gift | Thank You Note Due | Sent |
|------|-------------------|---------------------|--------------------|------|
|      |                   |                     |                    |      |
|      |                   |                     |                    |      |
|      |                   |                     |                    |      |
|      |                   |                     |                    |      |
|      |                   |                     |                    |      |
|      |                   |                     |                    |      |
|      |                   |                     |                    |      |
|      |                   |                     |                    |      |
|      |                   |                     |                    |      |

## *Gifts Received / Thank You Notes Sent*

| Date | Who Gave the Gift | Description of Gift | Thank You Note Due | Sent |
|------|-------------------|---------------------|--------------------|------|
|      |                   |                     |                    |      |
|      |                   |                     |                    |      |
|      |                   |                     |                    |      |
|      |                   |                     |                    |      |
|      |                   |                     |                    |      |
|      |                   |                     |                    |      |
|      |                   |                     |                    |      |
|      |                   |                     |                    |      |
|      |                   |                     |                    |      |

## *Gifts Received / Thank You Notes Sent*

| Date | Who Gave the Gift | Description of Gift | Thank You Note Due | Sent |
|------|-------------------|---------------------|--------------------|------|
|      |                   |                     |                    |      |
|      |                   |                     |                    |      |
|      |                   |                     |                    |      |
|      |                   |                     |                    |      |
|      |                   |                     |                    |      |
|      |                   |                     |                    |      |
|      |                   |                     |                    |      |
|      |                   |                     |                    |      |
|      |                   |                     |                    |      |
|      |                   |                     |                    |      |

## Gifts Received / Thank You Notes Sent

| Date | Who Gave the Gift | Description of Gift | Thank You Note Due | Sent |
|------|-------------------|---------------------|--------------------|------|
|      |                   |                     |                    |      |
|      |                   |                     |                    |      |
|      |                   |                     |                    |      |
|      |                   |                     |                    |      |
|      |                   |                     |                    |      |
|      |                   |                     |                    |      |
|      |                   |                     |                    |      |
|      |                   |                     |                    |      |
|      |                   |                     |                    |      |

# *Gifts Received / Thank You Notes Sent*

| Date | Who Gave the Gift | Description of Gift | Thank You Note Due | Sent |
|------|-------------------|---------------------|--------------------|------|
|      |                   |                     |                    |      |
|      |                   |                     |                    |      |
|      |                   |                     |                    |      |
|      |                   |                     |                    |      |
|      |                   |                     |                    |      |
|      |                   |                     |                    |      |
|      |                   |                     |                    |      |
|      |                   |                     |                    |      |
|      |                   |                     |                    |      |

## *Gifts Received / Thank You Notes Sent*

| Date | Who Gave the Gift | Description of Gift | Thank You Note Due | Sent |
|------|-------------------|---------------------|--------------------|------|
|      |                   |                     |                    |      |
|      |                   |                     |                    |      |
|      |                   |                     |                    |      |
|      |                   |                     |                    |      |
|      |                   |                     |                    |      |
|      |                   |                     |                    |      |
|      |                   |                     |                    |      |
|      |                   |                     |                    |      |
|      |                   |                     |                    |      |

## Gifts Received / Thank You Notes Sent

| Date | Who Gave the Gift | Description of Gift | Thank You Note Due | Sent |
|------|-------------------|---------------------|--------------------|------|
|      |                   |                     |                    |      |
|      |                   |                     |                    |      |
|      |                   |                     |                    |      |
|      |                   |                     |                    |      |
|      |                   |                     |                    |      |
|      |                   |                     |                    |      |
|      |                   |                     |                    |      |
|      |                   |                     |                    |      |
|      |                   |                     |                    |      |

## *Gifts Received / Thank You Notes Sent*

| Date | Who Gave the Gift | Description of Gift | Thank You Note Due | Sent |
|------|-------------------|---------------------|--------------------|------|
|      |                   |                     |                    |      |
|      |                   |                     |                    |      |
|      |                   |                     |                    |      |
|      |                   |                     |                    |      |
|      |                   |                     |                    |      |
|      |                   |                     |                    |      |
|      |                   |                     |                    |      |
|      |                   |                     |                    |      |
|      |                   |                     |                    |      |

## Gifts Received / Thank You Notes Sent

| Date | Who Gave the Gift | Description of Gift | Thank You Note Due | Sent |
|------|-------------------|---------------------|--------------------|------|
|      |                   |                     |                    |      |
|      |                   |                     |                    |      |
|      |                   |                     |                    |      |
|      |                   |                     |                    |      |
|      |                   |                     |                    |      |
|      |                   |                     |                    |      |
|      |                   |                     |                    |      |
|      |                   |                     |                    |      |
|      |                   |                     |                    |      |

## *Gifts Received / Thank You Notes Sent*

| Date | Who Gave the Gift | Description of Gift | Thank You Note Due | Sent |
|------|-------------------|---------------------|--------------------|------|
|      |                   |                     |                    |      |
|      |                   |                     |                    |      |
|      |                   |                     |                    |      |
|      |                   |                     |                    |      |
|      |                   |                     |                    |      |
|      |                   |                     |                    |      |
|      |                   |                     |                    |      |
|      |                   |                     |                    |      |
|      |                   |                     |                    |      |